I0493269

BECOME A MONEY MAKING MACHINE: HOW TO FIND FINANCIAL SUCCESS WITH AFFILIATE MARKETING

Daniel Shepherd

Income 4 Life

INTRODUCTION

There have been so many new and different types of marketing over the last decade or two, you may think that it is pointless for you to get familiar with what people are now claiming will really make you a lot of money. Buzz words in marketing have the same life span as the latest thing in technology, largely because marketing is so closely tied to technology. However, much of the dust has settled and affiliate marketing has been around long enough that people have come to realize the possibilities. The number of success stories demonstrates just how much potential there is in this type of marketing.

The thing to remember is that there is a right and many wrong ways to do it.

This book is designed to help you understand what affiliate marketing is, how it works, and the best way to implement it to succeed. It also looks at the most common mistakes that people make to negate all of the time and effort they put into it. The book also covers the myths and facts so that you can avoid things that don't work and so that you have realistic expectations before getting started.

Make sure to read this book all the way through before you get started. Unlike a lot of books, this book will help you to do it right, and help you to have an understanding of the concepts and execution that you need to know before you begin. Once you have completely read the book, you can go back through it and start working on your strategy.

Table of Contents

CHAPTER 1. WHAT IT IS AND WHAT IT ISN'T

The reason affiliate marketing can be such a great source of extra income is because you are helping to sell someone else's product. You can do this for products and services that you already enjoy and believe in, which means you can actually make money recommending something you are already giving positive reviews for any way. Companies will actually pay you if your recommendations result in a sale. All of your recommendations are tracked through the company whose products or services you are praising on your site. The link with your recommendation takes users to the product's site, and the company uses a unique code to track when links from your site result in a sale.

Yes, you are actually earning commissions by linking recommendations from your site to other company sites. If you have a site and are able to attract a good bit of traffic to it, you can make a bit of money from adding links to sites that you are already talking about in your regular content anyway.

Basically, you are able to make money doing something you are probably already doing. You can think of it as earning commission or as a referral fee, however you want to describe it.

It is a completely legitimate money-making method. You just need to contact the merchants you want to recommend and work through their affiliate program.

FINDING YOUR NICHE

Because affiliate marketing is based on your existing site (or sites), it means you are going to want to find niche affiliate programs that can be worked into your current discussions. You do <u>not</u> want to suddenly start trying to sell something that doesn't fit into the tone and style of your site.

Affiliate programs are meant to blend in so that they do not come across as obvious sales pitches. Merchants may not really care how you drive traffic to their site resulting in sales, but it will make a big difference to you and the people who go to your site. The more you make people feel like your webpages are all about sales, the less often they will visit. Instead of increasing sales to your site, you will lose the people who once enjoyed reading what you have to say.

If you run your own business, this is something you will really want to be careful about before adding to your site. While people are already coming to your site to shop, they may not be interested in being taken to another site because they may not be comfortable with paying for something on an unfamiliar site, no matter how familiar they are with your site. However, you can find ways of making the recommendation as part of a supplement to your product. Just make sure it is clear that you are sending them to a different site. As long as you are very clear about where they are being taken, people are much more likely to be alright with the switch. And if they aren't, they will know better than to click on the link.

NOT ADS

Affiliate marketing is not like a Google Ad. It does not involve popups or other annoying marketing strategies. Affiliate marketing should be built into your site as a link, although it should be clear that clicking on the link will cause the reader to leave the pages under your control. However, other than that, it should not come across as a sales pitch, or not too much as one.

You've probably seen more than enough of popup ads or other ads that interrupt the flow of articles and blogs. While you can do something like this, it is not nearly as likely to get you the returns you are looking for from your marketing strategy. If readers do follow the link on an ad, it is much more likely to be by accident, which will cause them to become frustrated or even angry. This is particularly likely from a mobile device where the pages take a little longer to load. When they try to scroll down, they may end up accidentally clicking on a link, which can make it a lot more difficult to return to the original page, particularly if the link is on one of your social media sites.

You want a more natural flow to your affiliate marketing to make the most of the links. The more organic the addition is, the more likely a person will be to consider actually following the link. People will be much more likely to trust your recommendations too if you don't come across as being a pushy sales person. Not only are they more likely to follow your affiliate link, they will be more likely to try to find other recommendations from you, whether through links on blogs or even email.

BE CAREFUL

Most importantly, affiliate marketing is not part of a scam. You should **_never_** pay someone to get you set up or to get started. Anyone who says that you need to invest in anything to be successful is a scam artist.

If you do not have a website, then you will need to invest in getting one established and start drawing in traffic, but that is not the same thing. Unless you are willing to dedicate the time and energy to learn how to maintain a website, it is going to cost you a bit to get set up.

Affiliate marketing is based on you already having the website. Before you can really turn affiliate marketing into a successful way to passively earn income, you need to establish your site. No amount of money can do this for you. If it could be done, marketers would be going directly to the people who are trying to sell you the idea.

Anyone saying they can help you get set up as an affiliate marketer for a fee is a scammer. You only need to work with the marketer directly to get established; you don't need a middle man. It's also a lot less work.

Chapter 2. Benefits and Potential

Affiliate marketing can be a good way to passively earn income, but there are benefits that go well beyond that. From strengthening partnerships to helping build your own site's exposure, you stand to benefit in a number of ways.

Building Stronger Partnerships

Affiliate marketing is about a lot more than simply earning extra money. It gives you a way to reach out to merchants and others in your niche market to start building a stronger connection to the community. These partnerships benefit both parties, financially and socially. It is possible that you will actually be able to pay your web hosting fees using the money you earn from your affiliations. At the same time, the merchant sees an increase in sales and positive reviews. This positive relationship builds trust and can help establish your site as more than just a place for occasional browsing.

KEEPING YOUR CONTENT FRESH

By working with a merchant, you will begin to look at your site from a different angle. You want to work links and ideas into your site that can easily flow into a recommendation for your affiliate.

This can be a double edged sword, so you will need to be careful. As mentioned in the previous chapter, you do not want your site to end up being just a big ad for other businesses. You need to keep the focus on the things that have hooked your existing audience. It is just that you are now also trying to assist that audience in finding things that they may also enjoy. Your blogs will take on a secondary purpose, as well as any videos and social media you use, keeping you looking at your information in a new light. The end result is that you will probably keep your content clearer and updated instead of letting things go stale.

IMPROVED TRACKING OF YOUR SITE

There are a lot of tools you can use to track metrics for your site, but affiliate marketing gives you a narrow focus on the income you earn without having to filter out everything else. You can get an idea of what pages with links are working to help bring in more income and which ones aren't. That gives you a way to reshape and improve your current strategy.

Since you will usually have more than one affiliate, you will also see which ones are working well for you and which affiliate links or suggestions could use a bit more work. It could be that your strategy for one particular recommendation is not gaining the attention for another type of audience.

BETTER MANAGEMENT OF YOUR TIME

As a result of better tracking, you will be able to y manage your time more effectively when you update your site, post blogs, or engage with your target audience. You will be able to see what trends are working to grow your traffic and which ones are on the decline. This means you will be able to cut out development on things that simply aren't working or when people are not interested.

It can also give you an idea of how people are reacting to different products and services based on what kind of links they are likely to follow. This will give you a strategy going forward to ensure that you keep your finger on the pulse of your target audience. Since you are probably already passionate about your site, this will be an extremely beneficial side effect of affiliate marketing.

INCREASED EXPOSURE

If you think that affiliate marketing primarily benefits your partner, you should examine the marketing method a little more closely. For every successful sale, you are increasing the value of your recommendations to your readers. More people will recommend your site, and the value of what you say will grow as a result. Word of mouth through comments and reviews is what really helps to increase traffic to affiliate sites as well. So if one of your regular visitors leaves a positive review for your partner, there is a good chance that that visitor is going to mention your site as being the place that brought his or her attention to the product or service. This will increase exposure for your site.

ADDITIONAL INCOME

Of course, the primary reason why people turn to affiliate marketing is it can be a fantastic way to earn extra income without having to dedicate hours to it every single week. As long as you remember to keep your content updated and include links to your affiliate periodically (you don't even have to do it every week, so long as you do add links to the affiliate at regular intervals), you can continue to make money without any other effort.

For a lot of social media savvy people, this is the real draw to affiliate marketing. If you already love and adore a product that you use, you probably talk about it with some regularity. Simply adding a link to your praise of a product or service does not take more than a minute of your time, but it can become a nice way to earn extra money. At a time when a lot of people are working multiple jobs, affiliate marketing can give you a way to turn your passion into actual income.

The more traffic you have to your site, the more potential you have. You do need to be realistic in your approach. If your site is part of a very small niche, you are not likely to earn a lot of income (although if what you earn is enough to cover the cost of your web-hosting, you are still gaining from the strategy without much effort). The bigger your online presence, the better your chances of turning your affiliate marketing into a real income.

CHAPTER 3. GETTING STARTED

Affiliate marketing starts with your website, interests, passions, and current audience. You should already have all of this established. Affiliate marketing works with this existing relationship and adds another layer of interaction – helping to sell the things you already use and love.

If you don't have a site, blog or newsletter already, you can include your marketing strategy into the site you do build, but that is well outside the scope of this ebook. That does not mean that it is a waste to read this book and understand marketing. It simply means that you have a lot more research and work to do before you can start earning a passive income from this type of marketing.

As long as you already have an online presence, you are ready to get started.

Your Resources

You don't have to have a website. If you maintain a blog, social media, or even just an email newsletter, you can become an affiliate marketer. Consider how you have talked about products and services in the past over your chosen medium. You will want to take a similar approach, at least initially. Since you haven't been tracking how many of your recommendations have created happy customers for these products, you won't yet know how well your recommendations paid off. However, it will be far less invasive to use what you have done in the past to keep the changes to a minimum.

Finding a Partner

There are a lot of different terms for the relationship, such as affiliate, partner, or marketer, but in the end it is a marketing partnership. Think of the items that you love and would like to see others enjoying. Create a list of companies that you think make fantastic products or offer outstanding services and tie in with your niche. Next, contact those companies and see if they have affiliate programs. If they do, you can start your relationship with them. This can take a while as you should contact several at a time. Each company has a process, and it could take a while to get everything established. This is a good thing because you will want to know that your partnership is properly set up before you start sending your audience to their site.

Most companies will have a link at the bottom of their website mentioning affiliates or affiliate programs, making it easy to determine what a company offers without having to call or email first. If you don't see something like that, you can use the contact information to call and ask, but it is always best to start by browsing their site. It will certainly be a much better start to the partnership.

Make sure you save the link they provide for use. You will _not_ be sending your followers through a normal link.

CONDUCTING RESEARCH

There are probably plenty of examples of sites, blogs, newsletters, and other online presences that are similar to yours. Take the time to research them to see how they manage their affiliate programs. You may find some highly creative methods that you can use or adjust to match your online presence. Perhaps there is a way to work a link onto most pages without making it into a blatant ad or burying it in blogs that move down in the search results over time.

There are also affiliate networks where you can get ideas and check into current campaigns. If the company or companies you are promoting have this kind of network, it can be a great place to build your presence and find a bigger audience for your own site, as well as getting ideas on how to better promote the company's products on your site.

WORKING YOUR LINKS INTO YOUR SITE

Working your new link into your site, newsletter, or social media account is completely up to you. The important thing to remember:

Use the affiliate link provided by the company.

You can add the link as a banner if you really want to highlight the product or service. You can dedicate an entire blog to a product or service the company offers. You can even mention it in passing on your Facebook account.

At this point, you should know your audience, so play to their interests. Build their curiosity or make a recommendation with conviction so that they will be more likely to try it out.

CONSIDER OTHER OFFERINGS FROM THE COMPANY

Once you are signed up as an affiliate, you don't have to try to sell just one product or service. If you are an avid fan of a company and you love multiple products by that company, you can regularly post links about something new you have tried, ask your audience what they think, or see who is interested in trying it out and weighing in for everyone else.

This is where keeping your site content fresh really comes into play. From the way you blog to the information you post in your newsletter, you will want to know what your partner company is doing so you can make recommendations when it makes sense. You don't want your audience to find out about something about an affiliate through another site.

Chapter 4. Building Long-Term Income

As mentioned in the previous chapters, this is not a get rich quick scheme. There is no promise of instant wealth, and certainly no guarantee that your affiliate marketing will end up making it possible for you to retire next year. That is not what affiliate marketing is about. In fact, I can promise you that if you don't put real time and energy into it, you won't get anything in return.

What affiliate marketing will do for you is to give you passive income. That means you will need to do a good bit of research before acting.

It is best if you already have a website that has traffic and you will be able to build your marketing strategy from there.

Develop Your Site

If you do not already have a site or if your site doesn't get much in the way of traffic, you will really need to start there. Unfortunately, this book is dedicated specifically to affiliate marketing, and it isn't possible to detail everything you need to do here. If you conduct a Google search for help developing your site and pulling in more traffic, you will find that you can get your site up and running in about 45 minutes. By the end of the week, you should start seeing improvements in the amount of traffic you receive. If you already have a site, you will need to start thinking about how to work affiliate marketing links into existing content (webpages, FAQs, and other static pages), as well as your blogs. It is much easier to update static content if you have already mentioned other companies or products. All you have to do is add the links to those comments or add the company (or specific goods or services you want to recommend) and then add the link. It really shouldn't take more than a couple of minutes, but it can quickly start having an effect .

It will be a little harder to work other companies in the blogs because your inclination will be to start turning them into sales pitches. Go through some of your recent blogs and look for places where you *could* have added your affiliate link. This will help you to keep the same tone and style that your current audience is used to seeing. Your readers will likely be curious as to where the link goes, and they are more likely to check it out and purchase something from your partner. They will be much more inclined to check it out than if you turn your blog into a blog-shaped ad.

RESEARCH

Taking care of your site is the easy part. The hard part is going to come when you start researching how others in your niche have managed to make it work. Perhaps they have actually dedicated an entire page on their site to affiliate marketing. If you do it right, this can actually be highly effective without giving the appearance that you are selling out your site. Affiliate marketing has been around long enough that people who understand how it works have been able to master it, turning it from a small passive income into a steady earner.

INITIAL RESEARCH

Take the time to see what these experts have done. Find discussion boards for your particular interests and see what people are saying about different products. See if affiliate marketing is discussed for your niche.

You can also check out boards specific to affiliate marketing, but this really isn't recommended. People are likely to be overstating their actual earnings or the potential of affiliate marketing. Even more likely, you'll encounter scammers who are trying to take advantage of those who are less sure of how it is done. This is why it is recommended that you work with sites specific to your interests. The people are more honest and open, and while they may not talk about affiliate marketing specifically, you can get a great idea of how sales pitches work with them, as well as the sites that they like. This kind of research is priceless.

MAINTAINING THE FEEL

To keep your passive income steady, you will need to maintain at least a monthly schedule for researching because you have to stay current with the way your field is going. You need to keep the same look and feel that has worked well in the past because a major shift is going to annoy your regular traffic. At the same time, you will need to incorporate new directions and ideas that are trending in your niche. This is how you can turn your initial success into something more.

ADD AFFILIATES

Once you become complacent with your current set up, your income is likely to plateau and then decline. Markets seldom stay the same, and that means you will need to continue to update your affiliations. It is very possible that you will continue to sell for some of your affiliates, but over time, you are likely to fall out of love with others. For example, the love of Beanie Babies came and went. While they are an interesting niche market, there have been many replacements for this kind of item, from other stuffed animals to things like the Tomodachi.

Then you have to consider that some of your affiliates may go out of business or drop their programs. This is why it is important to always know how things are going with your affiliates and to always be on the lookout for new ones as you find other things that you love and want to promote.

LOVE THE THINGS YOU PROMOTE

The most important way to turn your traffic into sales with your affiliates is to be honest and passionate about the things you have purchased from them. If you want to do this through a review section on your website, that can really help your sales.

However, the key is that you should only be promoting things you love and believe in. Your enthusiasm will come across in your posts, and that will make all the difference in the world. As people start to see the value of your recommendations, they will be much more likely to listen to you again in the future. This steady following is what will help you turn a small, infrequent income into something steady.

EVALUATE YOUR LINKS

No matter how much you love something, the way you sell it may simply fail to change people's opinions. Take the time to analyze your own links and see how well they have performed. The better the performance, the more confident you will be in your approach going forward.

Just like you have to maintain your website based on what is doing well and what isn't, you need to shift your affiliate marketing strategy to use what works and retire what doesn't.

Chapter 5. Tools

Before diving into tools, there's one thing you need to remember.

You shouldn't pay a cent to be an affiliate marketer.

This includes any tools you use. Don't be tricked into buying tools. There are more than enough free tools out there to make sure you can succeed by dedicating time, not money, in your marketing strategy.

Now that you've had that reminder, let's get you set up with some tools to turn your passive income into meaningful earnings.

Getting Ideas

No matter how long you have been maintaining your site, you will have times when it will be difficult to come up with new content ideas. There are several tools out there to help you narrow down what you should talk about on your site. Do keep in mind this does not help you work the links into your site; it helps you come up with ideas for blogs, webpages, or other content. From what's trending to idea generation, there are a number of tools to keep your content current and more attractive to potential visitors.

- Content Idea Generators asks you just under 20 questions about your field and returns ideas based on your answers. Even better, you can use content ideas for just about any kind of online information, from white-papers to videos, to press releases.

- Buzzsumo focuses on your subject and analyzes what the current Internet trends on the niche are. This can help you keep your blogs and news current so that your visitors will get the latest information. It can also give you a way to work in the newest products and services of your current affiliates. It may also give you ideas for other products and services for potential partners. It's a great way to expand the number of affiliates you have.

- Portent's Content Idea Generator takes your subject and gives you possible ideas. It may present ideas you have already used, but you can think of them from a different angle to maximize your site's viewership on trending topics. There are other tools at the bottom of the page to get you moving on other areas, so you can use this page to do more than just get ideas for content.

GETTING THE RIGHT HEADLINES

Once you have the right content, you need to make sure your headlines will get people's attention. One of the things you need to get working for you is your site, newsletter, or other type of headline. Here are a couple of tools you can use to help evaluate how your current headlines are working. The goal of your blog titles, webpages, and other headers is to increase how much traffic you get so that you can convert more visitors into buyers for your affiliates.

EMOTIONAL MARKETING VALUE HEADLINE ANALYZER

Emotional Marketing Value Headline Analyzer is a unique tool that will tell you what kind of emotions your headline evokes. All you have to do is enter your headline into the box and specify your industry. The program will provide a percentage score for the headline and detail what kind of emotion it evokes. The higher the percentage, the more likely it is that people will take the time to read what you have to say.

BLOG POST HEADLINE ANALYZER

The Blog Post Headline Analyzer is designed for blog posts since they are a regular part of site maintenance and information sharing/generating. This tool looks at a number of different areas to help you across the board: structure, grammar, and readability. It then helps you figure out where you can work to improve your headline's rating.

STAYING SEO CONSCIOUS

The best way to get traffic is to have your content appear on the first page of search engines, and that is done through SEO. Fortunately, there are a plethora of tools to improve your ranking with several of the search engines.

GOOGLE WEBMASTER TOOLS

As the biggest and most well-known search engine, Google has made it very easy for you to see how well your site is performing in its searches – Google Webmaster Tools. You should set aside a considerable amount of time to get familiar with all of their options. Once you know how to use them, you will be able to significantly increase the amount of traffic you get to your site, which will increase the likelihood that people will use your links and make purchases.

GOOGLE ANALYTICS

Like the webmaster tools, Google Analytics offers a large range of tools to see how well your site is doing to attract visitors. These tools are considerably different to the webmaster tools, so you should plan to spend a good bit of time on this site as well. Once you know how to use the tools, you will significantly increase the odds of having your webpages returned near the top of various types of queries.

MAJESTIC SEO

Majestic SEO is an independent tool that gives you a more objective look at your SEO rankings, regardless of the search engine a potential visitor uses. From details on how your profile is doing to details about keywords, this site can improve your overall Internet presence.

KEYWORD SPY

Keyword Spy is another independent site that helps to improve your site's performance. The analytic tools it offers can make your affiliate marketing strategy more competitive. And don't be fooled by the appearance and information – the trial is for a lifetime free period, so you won't have to pay for it. It will also help you if you are involved in pay per click advertising too.

Improving Your Social Media

To get the most out of links, you will want to include social media in your strategy. With so many people taking advice and recommendations from sites like Facebook and Twitter, you should consider managing a social media site if you aren't already. It will go a long way to increasing your traffic and your potential passive income. There are several tools that can give you a boost on social media.

- Followerwonk is a Twitter specific tool that can increase the number of followers you have. With so few characters, it is easy to post to Twitter and incorporate your links on a regular basis.

- Buffer gives you an advantage no matter which of the major social media sites you are managing. They cover the five biggest sites: Pintrest, Twitter, Facebook, Google+, and

Instagram. You can post what you would like to say that day, and Buffer will make it go live at the optimal time of the day, when people are more likely to be online. It can also post to multiple sites so that you can do all of your set up in a single location instead of having to log in to the different sites to manage them.

OPTIMIZING YOUR LINKS

To ensure your links are really working for you, take the time to get familiar with a couple of these tools and choose the one or two that really work for you.

GOOGLE'S URL BUILDER

If you are a fan of Google Analytics, Google's URL Builder is the perfect tool to analyze your links. It will track a wealth of your sites (such as social media) and let you know how the links and URLs are performing.

BIT.LY

One of the most popular link analyzers is independent – Bit.ly. It is incredibly popular because it is so easy to use and yet very useful in improving the way you link. It can take really lengthy link addresses and shorten them. It also tracks click information for your PDF and Kindle book link clicks, so you know if these links are working along with your site links.

CLICKMETER

Another completely free service, ClickMeter is specifically for affiliates. Both it and Linktrack are great tools for seeing how well your links are doing to drive your visitors to your affiliate sites. Take time to learn both of these so that you know which one works better for you. Then start really tracking the success of your links so you can duplicate the success in your future content.

Chapter 6. How to Do It Right

There are a lot of ways to be a successful affiliate marketer, and much depends on your niche. However, there are a few things that are virtually always true about the best in the business. The following suggestions will help you make sure all the work you have done to this point leads to a passive income that amounts to more than a little check at the end of the year.

Believe in Your Products

The best affiliate marketers are ardent supporters of the products they push. You've seen celebrities gushing about products on TV, or even just wearing something, and the product's sales go through the roof. Although your impact is considerably smaller, your audience clearly listens to what you have to say, and if you push a product or service that you haven't tried, or worse, one you don't like, you will lose your base audience. Your recommendations will become less credible and all that work will end up being wasted time.

Also, it is usually very clear when someone is really passionate about, or at least an ardent believer in, a particular product or service. If a reader comes back and says their experience was negative, you can make recommendations and give advice for alternative ways to do something. If you believe in the products your site leads to, you can have meaningful discussions, and that is much more likely to result in increased sales.

KEEP CONTACT WITH YOUR AFFILIATE COMPANIES

Take the time to look into new things they produce and sell. This allows you to recommend new goods and services, something that people will want to purchase after one or two successful experiences with other recommendations you have posted. And you won't need to do anything additional to sell the goods or services of a company that you are already affiliated with. The affiliate link is good for *anything* that the company sells. The agreement is a one-time requirement, so once it is in place, you are able to continually offer recommendations on other items or services if you try them and find you love them.

That is one reason it is important to research companies in the beginning. Find a company that consistently makes things you love and use, and then join their family as an affiliate marketer. It is meant to be a very positive, symbiotic relationship that benefits both of you. And it shouldn't feel like work. Because when you love something, you want to share it. Even if you end up only having one partner, if you choose wisely (based on a company you believe in and that is likely to keep making great stuff), by staying current on their products, you can make a nice income just by telling people how reliable they are.

KEEP IT RELEVANT

One of the worst things you can do is to come across as a marketer. Many of your readers are going to quickly tire of your sales pitch if you are blatantly selling. The most obvious way to come across as a marketer is to try to sell things that have no relevance to what your site is about.

If you have been losing weight and have attracted a large number of followers during your blogging, suddenly pushing your readers to try a new smartphone or car makes absolutely no sense whatsoever. You can talk about clothes you wear that make working out more comfortable, the kinds of foods and drinks that you find boosts your energy or metabolism, or even apps you use that help you stay focused. Don't just throw a sales pitch into the middle of your story and expect people to be interested. More likely they will find it a source of annoyance, and the more often you try it, the more readers you are going to lose.

There are always angles you can use to link to things you love, but always step back and ask if it makes sense for your niche market before you try it. If there is something you are really passionate about and you want to promote it, perhaps it is time to start a new site and direct your audience there. If they are interested in this change of topic, they can check out your new pages. If not, they can stick to the topic that drew them into your site.

Use the Tools and Experiment

There is always a better way to do something. Even if you find that your site is optimized for your affiliate income in the beginning, don't worry, that will change in a year's time because technology does not stay the same.

This is why it is so important to find the right tools for your needs and to play around with different techniques. This ensures that you get the most out of your affiliations, that your marketing strategy does not get stale, and that your passive income continues to improve over time.

Understand the Terms and Deals

Affiliate programs are numerous, and some companies have multiple agreements. It is very possible that by going through a different network, you will be able to earn more per sale from your site than through your existing network. Take the time to find out which affiliate program will earn you the most for something you are going to do any way. If a company pays 15% through one network and 25% through another, obviously you want to get set up through the network that pays out 25% for the same amount of work.

The other thing to check is the Terms of Service associated with each of your partners. If your primary audience is reached through email and newsletters, you won't want to use an affiliate program like Amazon Associates because they do not allow you to include affiliate links to your emails, not even attachments. You need to understand the fine print.

DISCLOSING YOUR CONNECTION

The last thing to look at is disclosures. It's not fun and you probably would prefer to ignore the subject entirely, but it is part of having an online presence and making money online.

Disclosures are essentially the fine print about using your site and links. It lets your readers know all of the points and details about the things you are helping sell so that they can make an informed decision.

But isn't it their job to understand that you are helping sell stuff? Don't you want to be aware when a site you read includes affiliate marketing?

That really depends on how you market your affiliate's merchandise. In 2013, the US Federal Trade Commission (FTC) updated rules and regulations on disclosure, and it applies to affiliate marketing. No matter how you feel about adding fine print, it's a requirement.

While you should take the time to see what applies to your particular niche by checking out the FTC's online guidelines on online disclosure, there are some universal elements to it.

1. Do not hide your disclosure or put it somewhere that it is likely to be missed. It needs to be an unavoidable part of the page.

2. Add the disclosure close to the link so it is nearly impossible to miss. Make sure there isn't a lot of stuff obscuring the fact that the link and disclosure are related. Also, do not have other links between the affiliate link and the disclosure as that could lead the potential buyer to another site before they actually read the disclosure.

3. Ensure that no other part of the site will cover the text, particularly popup ads or ads that can obscure parts of the page.

4. Adding a disclosure does not automatically meet the requirements. If it is located in a place

where readers are not likely to see it, if it is unclear that it goes to a particular link, or if it appears further down the page (the readers have to scroll to see it), you need to add something to attract their attention to the disclosure. This ensures that readers understand what is going on before they make a purchase after using your link.

Check out the FTC's page to see some excellent examples of what to do to add disclosures to your site or other online content.

CHAPTER 7. SPECIALIZATIONS AND BEST PERFORMERS

The truth about affiliate marketing is that some niches are just far more effective than others in terms of their potential. Whether because the target audience is more well-versed in online shopping, because the goods and services lend themselves to impulse purchases, or because your visitors are more likely to be in the market, there are some areas that do better.

The areas that do the best really shouldn't come as a surprise because they are the things that do well no matter what type of marketing you are doing. These three areas are basically staples of human existence:

- Money
- Relationships
- Health

All you have to do is look in your junk mail folder to see that these three areas are easily the most frequently forced on people. That's because these are the areas that people are usually looking to improve. A person is far more likely to make a purchase related to one of these areas than any other.

IMPLEMENT WITH CAUTION

Odds are you already have your site created and you love it, as do your readers. Trying to add these links into the mix may seem like a huge stretch. If there really is no way to work an affiliation for one of these into your site, then don't try it.

Forcing it will not benefit anyone.

Your audience is going to be annoyed with the sudden appearance of something totally unrelated to their reason for reading your site. Your partners will see that you are not contributing much. And you will have wasted a lot of time on something that failed to yield results.

FIND THE COMMONALITY

Keeping in mind you should not force things, you can probably find some way to work these three topics into your regular blogs or emails because money, relationships, and health are a part of everyday life. They are tied to virtually everything.

So if you find a financial app that really helps you, you can probably find a way to work it into your blog, especially if it is about self-improvement. If you have an incredibly positive experience with your insurance company, you can definitely gush about that without upsetting anyone (especially since people really have low expectations for insurance carriers and a positive story is going to be of interest). If you have recently had a really negative dating experience, you can work that into a blog, social media, or other area.

These three areas are considered universal for a reason – you experience them every single day. Money is the entire reason you are even reading this book. Health is something that is of constant concern once you reach your 30s or have kids (younger people don't tend to worry about it as much unless it is an issue). Of course weight loss and other appearance aspects fall under the health umbrella, making it one of the most publicized topics. Relationships are not limited to singles. Whether you are dating, in a stable relationship, married, or uninterested in having a romantic relationship, you still deal with relationships. Relationships go far beyond just romance – they cover all interactions with people. Advice on dealing with different personalities and problems at work may not be as popular as romantic engagements, but the number of people looking to improve even this kind of relationship is enormous.

GET EMOTIONAL

Whether or not you can work one of these areas into your site content, you need to show personality and emotion. Naturally, you don't want to go overboard with your emotion, but your sales pitches need to display a personality. It needs to be obvious that a person wrote it, someone who firmly believes in what they are saying.

During your research, you are going to find that the best performers are either specialized or their sales pitches have emotion to them.

Use unique words that get the point across about how you actually feel about a product. Common words should be used sparingly because that's what ads and obvious marketing do. Words like very, fantastic, amazing, and great have been used so often that people tend to take them with a grain of salt (if they bother to notice them at all). These words indicate you are trying to make a sale, not that you actually believe in what you are selling.

If you were talking to someone, what would you say to convince them that you actually love the product? Act as though you are talking to just your reader, and the emotions will immediately start to show in your content. It is this one-on-one relationship that readers love. If they feel like you are speaking to them, they are going to be more inclined to follow your link. The best way to do this is by using emotion in your work. People rarely get worked up or honestly emotional when speaking to crowds. The same is true of most sites. The content is professional and somewhat bland because of the lack of emotion.

Add a spark of emotion and you will find that you don't need to include those three specializations because people will be drawn to the fact that your site is unique.

CHAPTER 8. MYTHS AND THE COLD HARD FACTS

Like any new type of marketing, there have been a lot of myths and down right lies that are passed around, particularly by scammers. If you don't take the time to really analyze a trend, you can lose readers to your site or miss a perfect opportunity to gain exposure and additional income.

Now that you have an idea about what affiliate marketing is and how it works, you need to know how it can be used against you. Here are five of the biggest myths about affiliate marketing, and the actual truth.

GET RICH QUICK

By now you should be well aware that unless you win the lottery, there is no way to get rich quickly. Yes, affiliate marketing is passive income, but there is a lot of work involved upfront. While it has caught on, the reason it is rife with scammers is that people do not really understand how it works or what they have to do to ensure that the program works for them.

Some people begin to look into affiliate marketing and decide not to do it when they realize how much work it entails at the beginning. For a start, you will not be the only one marketing like this, and your competition already has a head start.

The difference is that you already have an audience. That is why it is so important to work the marketing into your current model without turning it into an obvious sales pitch. Especially in the early days, that means a good bit of work trying to figure out the right approach to keep your audience and still convince them to take a chance on the product or service.

You also have to foster a positive relationship with the company whose goods and services you are trying to sell. That also takes work and time.

AFFILIATE MARKETING ONLY WORKS FOR PARTICULAR NICHES

This idea is completely untrue (and those who believe it probably fell victim to a scam or thought that it was a way to get rich quick). Affiliate marketing works great in any industry for any niche as long as you do it right. If you don't exercise properly, you may believe that exercise only benefits a certain kind of person. It's the same thing for anything else. You have to do it in the right way to be successful.

When the niche that you market to matters is the type of approach you take to your strategy. Different personalities and industries are accustomed to and prefer a certain type of approach, which is why you really need to know who your audience is. You don't want to add marketing for a product that doesn't have anything to do with your website. This is just a way to annoy your audience with blatant marketing instead of your suggestion being a genuine way of trying to help your reader through that recommendation.

As you create your strategy, keep in mind who visits your site and what is likely to drive them to click on links. That is the best way to turn what some people consider a difficult marketing niche into a success story.

THE AFFILIATE MARKETING DOESN'T REALLY WORK ANYMORE

This myth is based on the changes Google made to their SEO algorithm a few years ago. It would be accurate to say that affiliate marketing doesn't work quite the same way as it did in the early days because of the change, but that does _not_ mean that it no longer works. Link building is always a bit tenuous anyway (kind of like keyword stuffing that resulted in really lousy content in the early days of the Internet).

The change to the algorithm had the same effect – it forced people to really consider how and when they linked instead of just cramming links onto a webpage. What the change highlights is the need for you to stay current on the latest SEO trends so that you can maximize how effective your links are. It should not discourage you from using affiliate marketing. If you stay up on the latest changes and trends, you will actually gain an advantage over your competition.

You Need to Spend Money to Make Money

This supposition is absolutely false when it comes to affiliate marketing, and it is a sign that you are dealing with a scam. Companies are looking for ways to drive traffic to their site – that means they are trying to get people to add links to their site. Companies are not going to make you pay to add links that drive traffic to their site.

Affiliate marketing requires no third party for it to work. It is a partnership between you and the business you are promoting. If you add any additional layers, you are making it into something that it is not meant to be, and that is what scammers are banking on. They will promise to help you earn more, but first you have to pay them.

Don't do it.

Everything about affiliate marketing is tied directly to your site. No one knows your site better than you, and no one else is going to be able to write in your voice or tone better than you (or whomever is currently writing for you). Paying someone to help you doesn't make any sense because there is nothing that anyone else can do better than you in this instance. You need to take the time to find out about the affiliate programs for the products you would like to promote, and no one is going to be able to represent you to the business better than you can.

Again, it comes down to you putting the effort and work in up front and making your own decisions. This isn't something you can pay someone else to do and have better results. Businesses will be more likely to value your relationship if you stay engaged with them as well, so make sure to put your best face forward.

CHAPTER 9. MISTAKES TO AVOID

Before you get started on updating your sites, there are a few things you should avoid. It is incredibly easy to make mistakes when marketing, and this is particularly true with affiliate marketing. You've already read about the things you should do, but there is nothing quite like learning about the mistakes of others to help you do a better job of understanding the right way to do something.

To assist you in getting a better start, here are some of the most common mistakes that affiliate marketers make. Keep in mind, you can make these mistakes (and are actually more likely to make them) after you've been doing affiliate marketing for a while. Bookmark this chapter and re-read it at least once a year to remind yourself that you should be avoiding these mistakes. Avoiding complacency is one of the best ways to be successful.

FAILING TO TEST THE LINKS

This should be a novice mistake, but it isn't. It doesn't matter how long you have been an affiliate marketer, if you don't test your site and the process that your links lead to, you are opening yourself up to all kinds of criticism and potentially losing many of your followers.

Testing links on your site should be second nature. If it isn't, you should minimize this ebook and do that right now. Visitors do not want to deal with broken links. It says that you really don't care if they actually can access what you are recommending or not. If they are really interested and your link doesn't work, they may google the item or service, and you won't get a cent out of them following your recommendation. You should also try the process yourself. Every time you join a new partner, make sure you go through all of the steps that your link takes your visitors through.

If there are any issues or things that aren't clear, you will be able to request they be fixed. Until they are fixed, you will be able to steer your visitors through the process. It shows you really do care, and that will make a positive impression.

HAVING TOO MANY

This refers to both having too many links on the page (your site isn't Amazon, so people don't want to be inundated with links – they aren't visiting to shop) and too many affiliates to track.

If you go from having none or just a couple links on your pages to having a page that is covered in links, people are going to become annoyed. First, there is no way that all of the products are relevant. Second, people will start to think you are too pushy and that your recommendations can be bought (even though that isn't true since affiliate marketers aren't bought).

It is also likely you will be too zealous when you first start. Don't let that lead to having far more partners than you could possibly use. You are not that passionate about that many products and services, so don't try to blanket your site with options that you can't honestly sell through enthusiasm. You know that you have too many partners when you can't manage them properly. If you can't figure out how much your links earn you in less than 10 minutes, you probably have too many affiliates.

Choose your partners based on quality, not quantity.

FAILING TO TRACK AND COMPARE

This one seems like it should be common sense, but all too often people do not bother to track their earnings or compare the products to those of the competition.

The first problem is easy to avoid by adding unique tracking links to each page, blog, email, or post. It really doesn't take you any longer to do this, and the benefits are important. Being able to see what is and is not working is essential in marketing, so why people make this mistake is a bit baffling.

Make sure you can identify the pages, posts, and emails that are earning you commission so that you can build strategies that work.

If you are tracking but aren't seeing improvements, odds are that your sales pitches are falling on deaf ears. If you are trying to push something in a saturated market, you *have* to know about the competition. Read up on other companies that are making similar products and why people love them. You can then make an entire page comparing what you love versus the competition, which will give you a way to add links, give you a topic to discuss (which is very nice if you are short on ideas), and increase your SEO because you are talking about a product that is currently trending.

LOSING YOUR HONESTY AND INTEGRITY

This one can be tough because it is possible and it can work against you. And that's actually the point. You may have loved your new printer for the first three months, but then it stopped working. Post an update about the printer warning people of the issues you encountered. If you found solutions, post those too. If you stay honest and open about your experience, it may end up being a short-term loss and a very long term gain. It is far too easy to be the sales person looking out for number one instead of the confidant or friend looking out for others.

Losing Focus

This ties into many of the other mistakes, but is unique in that you are guaranteed to do it at some point. You will be praising a product, then suddenly you'll find something else you love more. This leads to sudden silence, which will make people question how much you actually loved the product you used to praise. If you come across as easily distracted, your recommendations will be far less appealing. If people take the time and energy to purchase something that you recommend, they want to know that it is going to keep them happy for a while. If it can't keep your attention, why should they bother?

Putting the Sale First

It is easy to turn into the person who starts a site with the intention of helping others or spreading the word and ending up no more than another sales person trying to make a buck.

This is the fastest way to lose your audience because, again, they do not come to your site to buy stuff. If that was their goal, they would be looking at Amazon, eBay, or some other site instead. If you come across as a sales person instead of someone who genuinely wants to help them, they are not going to keep coming back to your site, read your emails, or follow you on social media.

Remember, you are making recommendations. Leave the obvious sales pitches to the company. You should be extolling the benefits and reasons that you absolutely love the product. If you don't love it, don't try to sell it.

Chapter 10. Tips & Tricks

When it comes to affiliate marketing, there is a lot to learn. Of course there are things you should do when you are just getting started and things you should always avoid, but what about the little things that can help boost your income? Of course, there are a few tips and tricks that can help you do it better, faster, and smarter.

Set a Google Alert for New Affiliate Programs

Google Alerts can let you know when a new program opens up in your niche. It's a tool, but one that is outside of the tools discussed in Chapter 5. This tool is specific to helping you grow your existing partnerships, but it keeps you focused on your niche. This can be a huge windfall when something new and interesting comes out and there is very little information about it online. Get the product or service. If you love it, join the program.

If you are an avid lover of a company and they don't currently have an affiliate program, this can let you know as soon as they begin one. It keeps you from having to remember to visit their site periodically. Google Alerts is free and easy to use. Take a few minutes to get familiar with what it has to offer and to set up an alert or two. Once you have a feel for how it works, you'll be able to dive in and really focus on companies that offer goods or services that you can really get enthusiastic about using.

AVOID DUPLICATING CONTENT

You should never copy/paste content straight from another source. Nor should you copy/paste content on your own page, or between your blogs and your newsletters, or anything else.

You should always have fresh content. Paraphrasing and summarizing are perfectly acceptable, but content that is identical is a really bad idea. And if you don't already feel guilty about doing it, Google's Panda search filter has another way to penalize you.

This particular search filter analyzes sites based on their content and if your site has too little content or duplicates content, it will rank you lower.

The reason this matters to you as an affiliate marketer is because it is very tempting to use what other people say or the text provided by the company itself. The end result is your content is not unique, and you will end up suffering for it.

And honestly, if you are really passionate about the product you won't be copying the content from somewhere else anyway. Your love for the product is unique, so show it in what you say.

KEEP LEARNING

Learn from your mistakes. Learn from the competition. Learn from what you are doing right. Learn from the experiences of others in other niches. Marketing is a highly competitive field, but affiliate marketing is unique. You aren't selling something based on the paycheck, you are selling it because it is something you use and love. This gives you an edge over other kinds of marketing because you are already familiar with the product or service; you know the ups and downs. You have already learned how to get the most out of it.

But there is always more to learn.

Don't let complacency and a couple of large earnings make you feel that you have finally reached success. Take them as vindication that others agree, and strive to learn more about similar products so you can become the authoritative voice.

ADD PRODUCT REVIEWS

This may seem like an easy way to identify a sales blog or email, but if you do it correctly, reviews are actually one of the best ways of selling people on a product. That means you have to mention the pros and the cons of the product. Nothing is perfect, so don't try to pitch something like it is perfect. Point out areas where you would like to see it grow or improve. This lets people know exactly what to expect, how to plan to implement the product or service, and request the same changes. Yes, it does mean if you bring up a point, more people are likely to lobby the company for the same things you want to see improved or added, and that can only make you love it more.

Avoid Linking in Every Page

If you add links to every page or social media post, you start to look more like a sales person than a person interested in the topic at hand. Emails are unique, and it is likely people will expect links, but do avoid over stuffing the emails with this cheap way to increase your passive income.

Remember, you are interested in helping people, and not just your bottom line.

Give It Time

The best advice is probably that it is going to take time, so be patient. If you are starting a site, it's going to take a while to build the traffic. If your site, newsletter, or other online presence was established a while back, it is going to take some time for people to start thinking of it as a way to find products and services that they can enjoy.

Nothing is a success overnight. Anything that is going to make you money is going to take work and time to catch on and actually work in your favor. You will want to turn all of that time you spent on research and updates into income, but you should know going in that it is going to take time for it to pay off. The longer you stick with it and the more you learn about how to market to your audience, the more passive income you will make.

Ultimately, it's a learning process that evolves over time. If you continue to build and grow your strategy based on what you find works for you, it can become a steady, healthy income.

Thank you for downloading and reading this book. I hope you found it useful and would love if you left comments for future improvements to the book and details about what you found most useful.

If affiliate marketing doesn't seem like the right source of extra income, you can check out some other ways to make money on the side on my website. From new releases to free content, the site is frequently updated to help you earn money in your spare time.